Sacred Ground

SACRED GROUND

A TRIBUTE TO AMERICA'S VETERANS

TOM RUCK

God Bless America!

Tony

Since 1947
**REGNERY
PUBLISHING, INC.**
An Eagle Publishing Company • Washington, DC

Cataloging-in-Publication data on file with the Library of Congress

ISBN 978-1-59698-524-7

Published in the United States by
Regnery Publishing, Inc.
One Massachusetts Avenue, NW
Washington, DC 20001
www.regnery.com

Manufactured in the United States of America

10 9 8 7 6 5 4 3 2 1

Books are available in quantity for promotional or premium use. Write to Director of
Special Sales, Regnery Publishing, Inc., One Massachusetts Avenue NW, Washington,
DC 20001, for information on discounts and terms or call (202) 216-0600.

DEDICATION

—⁘—

FIRST AND FOREMOST THIS BOOK IS DEDICATED TO EVERY MAN AND WOMAN who has, who is currently, and who will proudly wear the uniform of our great country. Without them, so many freedoms we take for granted would not be possible.

To the three greatest parents a son could ever have. My fathers Joseph Ruck and Stanley Lay who taught me so much and had so much more to give each one of us, and in many ways still continue to give, day in and day out. To my mom Eleanor Lay, a one-of-a-kind woman whose love and spirit will never be matched. How she loved living, her family, and her friends. All three of my parents loved to love everything that life could give and embraced it with such passion. They believed in America and the American dream and worked hard every day of their lives pursuing that dream. It is still amazing to me how much they continually gave of themselves to make others happy. They are remembered and missed by many because of the life they led and the life that they gave. To paraphrase my stepfather, "They were the most, to say the least." I am honored that they are at their final resting place at Jefferson Barracks National Cemetery in St. Louis, Missouri.

To my "Uncle Brother" (Charles Trokey), who lives life to the fullest and is a true example of how one should live his life. A truly unique and one-of-a-kind gentlemen of compassion, caring, faith, and humor who has always been there for so many of us.

And finally, to Ralph Smith. Ralph is a man of the people who has served the state of Missouri proudly in many capacities (executive assistant to Governors Bond and Ashcroft, state tax commissioner, and the Missouri Farm Bureau, just to mention a few). His guidance towards life and the way it should be lived was simple and his character was never questioned. Thank you for taking the time to let me listen to you on life and how we should take responsibility for our lives and to make sure we live it to the fullest.

Seven Pines National Cemetery, Sandston, Virginia

Contents

—◦ᴗ◦◆◦ᴗ◦—

CONTENTS

Introduction
Tom Ruck

ALONE, WE STAND AS THE SHINING BEACON OF LIBERTY AND FREEDOM TO the world. The freedoms we enjoy today have not come without a price and are too often taken for granted. Because of the brave men and women—who, from the very start of our nation's existence, have worn the uniform of all branches of the military so we can live in freedom without fear—we have the freedom to worship as we choose; vote as we choose; travel from one end of this great country to the other; and the opportunity to succeed or fail in pursuing our own individual versions of the American dream.

Every American, especially our children, needs to understand and embrace the sacrifices of our soldiers, sailors, airmen, guardsmen, and marines—and most importantly, what their families have endured, all to help preserve the promise of the American dream.

At a military cemetery, there is no differentiation of politics, rank, color, or gender—just men and women who had the honor to wear the uniform of the United States of America. For it is at this final resting place that one of our Founding Fathers' principles, "All Men Are Created Equal," truly comes to life.

This book is dedicated to those Americans who, at a moment's notice, knew that they might be put into harm's way to protect the American dream and the American way of life. We are the "land of the free" because we are the "home of the brave." To those of every generation who made that commitment, the commitment to duty, honor, and country, we say: Thank you!

Los Angeles National Cemetery, Los Angeles, California

FOREWORD
BOB DOLE

AMERICA REMEMBERS ITS VETERAN SONS AND DAUGHTERS WITH A FINAL resting place of respect, honor, and dignity they so rightly deserve. Americans who answered the call to duty and proudly wore the uniform of our great country will be remembered for all time at our national cemeteries.

Our national cemeteries are rich with the history of past and current generations who understood the meaning of liberty and the dangerous task of defending it. From those who fought for the birth of our nation to the men and women in uniform who are fighting at this moment, America has never stopped taking a stand against our enemies. The cost of freedom and liberty is high, and the courage to sustain it, even greater.

Many take our way of life for granted and lose sight of the fact that America continues to pay a price to remain a great country. The sacrifices made by heroic men and women from all walks of life to keep our society free and full of endless opportunities are an inspiration to all.

I encourage you to visit one of our national cemeteries. Take your children and grandchildren along so they will begin to understand the responsibility we all have to keep America as strong and free as it is today. While there, say a prayer for those who fought and died for us. These cemeteries remind us that at some time in our own lives, we may be called upon to sacrifice for our country to preserve our freedoms and liberties.

As you turn the pages of *Sacred Ground*, view the magnificent photographs of these resting places of honor; I am certain you will leave with a new sense of understanding of the reverence toward our military veterans, the bravest and truest patriots.

FLORIDA NATIONAL CEMETERY, BUSHNELL, FLORIDA

THE SOUTH

"But in a larger sense, we cannot dedicate, we cannot consecrate, we cannot hallow this ground. The brave men, living and dead, who struggled here, have consecrated it, far above our poor power to add or to detract. The world will little note nor long remember what we say here, but it can never forget what they did here."

—*Abraham Lincoln,*
Gettysburg Address, November 19, 1863

BARRANCAS NATIONAL CEMETERY, PENSACOLA, FLORIDA

"*Let us cross over the river*
and rest under the shade of trees."

—Thomas "Stonewall" Jackson

FORT BLISS NATIONAL CEMETERY, EL PASO, TEXAS

* * *

"There is a true glory and a true honor:

the glory of duty done, the honor of integrity of principle."

—ROBERT E. LEE

Douglas MacArthur
Excerpt from Thayer Award
Acceptance Address

May 12, 1962
West Point, New York

THAT I SHOULD BE INTEGRATED IN THIS WAY WITH SO NOBLE AN IDEAL arouses a sense of pride and yet of humility which will be with me always: Duty, Honor, Country.

… Unhappily, I possess neither that eloquence of diction, that poetry of imagination, nor that brilliance of metaphor to tell you all that they mean. The unbelievers will say they are but words, but a slogan, but a flamboyant phrase. Every pedant, every demagogue, every cynic, every hypocrite, every troublemaker, and I am sorry to say, some others of an entirely different character, will try to downgrade them even to the extent of mockery and ridicule.

But these are some of the things they do. They build your basic character…. They create in your heart the sense of wonder, the unfailing hope of what next, and the joy and inspiration of life. They teach you in this way to be an officer and a gentleman.

And what sort of soldiers are those you are to lead? Are they reliable? Are they brave? Are they capable of victory? Their story is known to all of you. It is the story of the American man-at-arms. My estimate of him was formed on the battlefield many, many years ago, and has never changed. I regarded him then as I regard him now—as one of the world's noblest figures, not only as one of the finest military characters, but also as one of the most stainless. His name and fame are the birthright of every American citizen. In his youth and strength, his love and loyalty, he gave all that mortality can give.

He needs no eulogy from me or from any other man. He has written his own history and written it in red on his enemy's breast. But when I think of his patience under adversity, of his courage under fire, and of his modesty in victory, I am filled with an emotion of admiration I cannot put into words. He belongs to history as furnishing one of the greatest examples of successful patriotism. He belongs to posterity as the instructor of future generations in the principles of liberty and freedom. He belongs to the present, to us, by his virtues and by his achievements. In twenty campaigns, on a hundred battlefields, around a thousand campfires, I have witnessed that enduring fortitude, that patriotic self-abnegation, and that invincible determination which have carved his statue in the hearts of his people. From one end of the world to the other he has drained deep the chalice of courage.

I do not know the dignity of their birth, but I do know the glory of their death.

They died unquestioning, uncomplaining, with faith in their hearts, and on their lips the hope that we would go on to victory.

BARRANCAS NATIONAL CEMETERY, PENSACOLA, FLORIDA

Always, for them: Duty, Honor, Country; always their blood and sweat and tears, as we sought the way and the light and the truth.

And twenty years after, on the other side of the globe, again the filth of murky foxholes, the stench of ghostly trenches, the slime of dripping dugouts; those boiling suns of relentless heat, those torrential rains of devastating storms; the loneliness and utter desolation of jungle trails; the bitterness of long separation from those they loved and cherished; the deadly pestilence of tropical disease; the horror of stricken areas of war; their resolute and determined defense, their swift and sure attack, their indomitable purpose, their complete and decisive victory— always victory. Always through the bloody haze of their last reverberating shot, the vision of gaunt, ghastly men reverently following your password of: Duty, Honor, Country.

...The soldier, above all other men, is required to practice the greatest act of religious training—sacrifice.

In battle and in the face of danger and death, he discloses those divine attributes which his Maker gave when he created man in his own image. No physical courage and no brute instinct can take the place of the Divine help which alone can sustain him.

GLENDALE NATIONAL CEMETERY,
RICHMOND, VIRGINIA

However horrible the incidents of war may be, the soldier who is called upon to offer and to give his life for his country is the noblest development of mankind.

...Today marks my final roll call with you, but I want you to know that when I cross the river, my last conscious thoughts will be of The Corps, and The Corps, and The Corps.

✳ ✳ ✳

"Of the marines at Iwo Jima,

uncommon valor was

a common virtue."

—CHESTER W. NIMITZ

SALISBURY NATIONAL CEMETERY, SALISBURY, NORTH CAROLINA

Barrancas National Cemetery, Pensacola, Florida

Hampton National Cemetery,
Hampton, Virginia

Seven Pines National Cemetery,
Sandston, Virginia

Salisbury National Cemetery, Salisbury, North Carolina
(Previous Spread): Arlington National Cemetery, Arlington, Virginia

* * *

"God bless them all! That's why we're here, to show our appreciation."

—Toby Keith

Thomas Paine
Excerpt from *The Crisis*

December 23, 1776

These are the times that try men's souls. The summer soldier and the sunshine patriot will, in this crisis, shrink from the service of their country; but he that stands by it now, deserves the love and thanks of man and woman. Tyranny, like hell, is not easily conquered; yet we have this consolation with us, that the harder the conflict, the more glorious the triumph. What we obtain too cheap, we esteem too lightly: it is dearness only that gives every thing its value. Heaven knows how to put a proper price upon its goods; and it would be strange indeed if so celestial an article as freedom should not be highly rated . . . .

As I was with the troops at Fort Lee, and marched with them to the edge of Pennsylvania, I am well acquainted with many circumstances, which those who live at a distance know but little or nothing of . . . .

Beaufort National Cemetery, Beaufort, South Carolina

Not a man lives on the continent but fully believes that a separation must some time or other finally take place, and a generous parent should have said, "If there must be trouble, let it be in my day, that my child may have peace"; and this single reflection, well applied, is sufficient to awaken every man to duty. Not a place upon earth might be so happy as America.

Wars, without ceasing, will break out till that period arrives, and the continent must in the end be conqueror; for though the flame of liberty may sometimes cease to shine, the coal can never expire.

I love the man that can smile in trouble, that can gather strength from distress, and grow brave by reflection. 'Tis the business of little minds to shrink; but he whose heart is firm, and whose conscience approves his conduct, will pursue his principles unto death....

Twice we marched back to meet the enemy, and remained out till dark. The sign of fear was not seen in our camp.... Once more we are again collected and collecting; our new army at both ends of the continent is recruiting fast, and we shall be able to open the next campaign with sixty thousand men, well armed and clothed. This is our situation, and who will may know it. By perseverance and fortitude we have the prospect of a glorious issue....

FLORIDA NATIONAL CEMETERY,
BUSHNELL, FLORIDA

* * *

"That was not the biggest battle that ever was, but for me it always typified one thing:

the dash, the ingenuity, the readiness at the first opportunity

that characterizes the American soldier."

—DWIGHT D. EISENHOWER

Hampton National Cemetery, Hampton, Virginia

✷ ✷ ✷

"You gain strength, courage, and confidence by every experience in which you really stop to look fear in the face."

—ELEANOR ROOSEVELT

BUZZ ALDRIN

March 2007

ONE OF THE MOST DEFINING MOMENTS IN MY LIFE WAS THAT FIRST STEP I took on the surface of the moon. Without the training and experience I gained from my career in the U.S. Air Force, I could never have taken it. Like many of my NASA colleagues, I had a career in the military before becoming an astronaut. After graduation from West Point, I went to Korea and was assigned to fly the F86 fighter jet. What I remember most about my time in Korea was the camaraderie and spirit of the men. These were men from all walks of American life who came together with a purpose and a mission, bonded by common values: duty, honor, and their love of family and country. In other words, the American way of life.

During my flight on Gemini 12 in 1966, had we lifted off on the day originally scheduled, my Extra Vehicular Activity (EVA), or space walk, would have taken

SOUTH FLORIDA VA NATIONAL CEMETERY, LAKE WORTH, FLORIDA
(OPPOSITE): FLAG CEREMONY AT BARRANCAS NATIONAL CEMETERY, PENSACOLA, FLORIDA

place on Veterans Day. I had brought along a Veterans Day pennant because I intended to cast it into space as a tribute to the memory of the men who had lost their lives in the service of their country. It was, I thought, an appropriate gesture. I said these brief words, "I'd like to extend the meaning of it to all the peoples of the world who have been, who are now, and will continue to strive for peace and freedom in the world," let go of the pennant, and watched it drift out into the blackness of space. I knew my words were being broadcast directly from Houston to the entire world, and it felt good to say thank you for so much to so many.

After my walk on the moon during the Apollo 11 mission in 1969 and the media frenzy that followed, there came the reality of having to become a real person again, and to get on with a normal life. I am very proud of the fact that one endeavor my whole family became involved with was the Voice in Vital America organization (VIVA), which supported those missing in action and prisoners of the Vietnam War in Southeast Asia. All five of us wore the POW/MIA bracelets proudly and of the five we wore, three were released, and my good friend Sam Johnson was one of them. We sent a plaque to each soldier which contained, along with a photograph of the moon, a small American flag and an Apollo 11 patch that I had taken to the moon. At the bottom of the plaque was a bracelet with the person's name and capture and release dates. Those brave men will always have a special place in my heart.

MARIETTA NATIONAL CEMETERY, MARIETTA, GEORGIA

All too often we take our freedom for granted. At times we forget that extraordinary men and women have sacrificed so much so that all of us may enjoy the freedoms we have. To all those who gave of themselves to preserve our way of life, the American way of life, I say: *thank you.*

(OPPOSITE): ARLINGTON NATIONAL CEMETERY, ARLINGTON, VIRGINIA

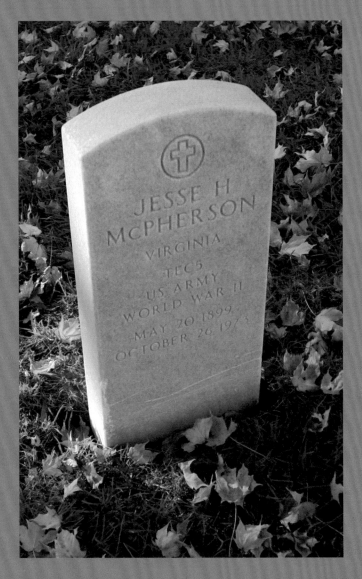

JESSE H
MCPHERSON

VIRGINIA

TEC5
US ARMY
WORLD WAR II
MAY 20 1899
OCTOBER 26 1973

Salisbury National Cemetery,
Salisbury, North Carolina

Marietta National Cemetery,
Marietta, Georgia

✳ ✳ ✳

"I have nothing to offer but blood, toil, tears, and sweat."

—Winston Churchill

✳ ✳ ✳

"We dare not forget that we are the heirs of that first revolution."

—JOHN F. KENNEDY

ARLINGTON NATIONAL CEMETERY, ARLINGTON, VIRGINIA

Barrancas National Cemetery, Pensacola, Florida

Richmond National Cemetery, Richmond, Virginia

Beaufort National Cemetery, Beaufort, South Carolina

The Battle Hymn of the Republic

Julia Ward Howe, December 1861

Mine eyes have seen the glory of the coming of the Lord;

He is trampling out the vintage where the grapes of wrath are stored;

He hath loosed the fateful lightning of His terrible swift sword;

His truth is marching on.

Glory! Glory! Hallelujah! Glory! Glory! Hallelujah!

Glory! Glory! Hallelujah! His truth is marching on.

I have seen Him in the watch fires of a hundred circling camps.

They have builded Him an altar in the evening dews and damps;

I can read His righteous sentence by the dim and flaring lamps;

His day is marching on.

Glory! Glory! Hallelujah! Glory! Glory! Hallelujah!

Glory! Glory! Hallelujah! His day is marching on.

I have read a fiery Gospel writ in burnished rows of steel;

"As ye deal with My condemners, so with you My grace shall deal";

Let the Hero, born of woman, crush the serpent with His heel,

Since God is marching on.

Glory! Glory! Hallelujah! Glory! Glory! Hallelujah!

Glory! Glory! Hallelujah! Since God is marching on.

He has sounded forth the trumpet that shall never call retreat;

He is sifting out the hearts of men before His judgment seat;

Oh, be swift, my soul, to answer Him! Be jubilant, my feet;

Our God is marching on.

Glory! Glory! Hallelujah! Glory! Glory! Hallelujah!

Glory! Glory! Hallelujah! Our God is marching on.

In the beauty of the lilies Christ was born across the sea,

With a glory in His bosom that transfigures you and me:

As He died to make men holy, let us live to make men free;

While God is marching on.

Glory! Glory! Hallelujah! Glory! Glory! Hallelujah!

Glory! Glory! Hallelujah! While God is marching on.

He is coming like the glory of the morning on the wave,

He is wisdom to the mighty, He is honor to the brave;

So the world shall be His footstool, and the soul of wrong His slave,

Our God is marching on.

Glory! Glory! Hallelujah! Glory! Glory! Hallelujah!

Glory! Glory! Hallelujah! Our God is marching on.

HOUSTON NATIONAL CEMETERY, HOUSTON, TEXAS

Fort Harrison National Cemetery, Richmond, Virginia

FLORIDA NATIONAL CEMETERY, BUSHNELL, FLORIDA

* * *

"It doesn't take a hero to order men into battle.
It takes a hero to be one of those men who goes into battle."

—NORMAN SCHWARZKOPF

33

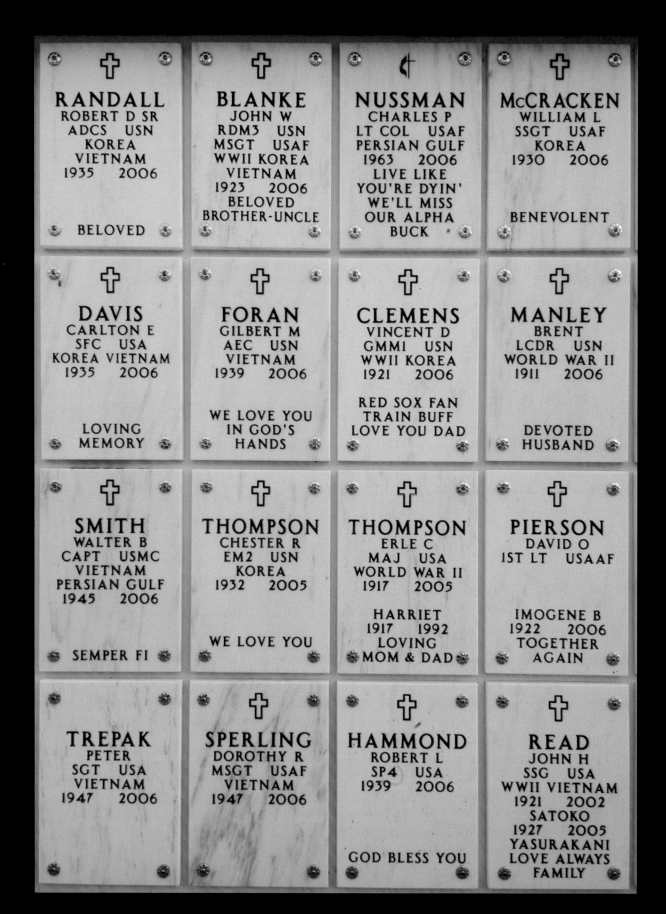

RANDALL
ROBERT D SR
ADCS USN
KOREA
VIETNAM
1935 2006

BELOVED

BLANKE
JOHN W
RDM3 USN
MSGT USAF
WWII KOREA
VIETNAM
1923 2006
BELOVED
BROTHER-UNCLE

NUSSMAN
CHARLES P
LT COL USAF
PERSIAN GULF
1963 2006
LIVE LIKE
YOU'RE DYIN'
WE'LL MISS
OUR ALPHA
BUCK

McCRACKEN
WILLIAM L
SSGT USAF
KOREA
1930 2006

BENEVOLENT

DAVIS
CARLTON E
SFC USA
KOREA VIETNAM
1935 2006

LOVING
MEMORY

FORAN
GILBERT M
AEC USN
VIETNAM
1939 2006

WE LOVE YOU
IN GOD'S
HANDS

CLEMENS
VINCENT D
GMM1 USN
WWII KOREA
1921 2006

RED SOX FAN
TRAIN BUFF
LOVE YOU DAD

MANLEY
BRENT
LCDR USN
WORLD WAR II
1911 2006

DEVOTED
HUSBAND

SMITH
WALTER B
CAPT USMC
VIETNAM
PERSIAN GULF
1945 2006

SEMPER FI

THOMPSON
CHESTER R
EM2 USN
KOREA
1932 2005

WE LOVE YOU

THOMPSON
ERLE C
MAJ USA
WORLD WAR II
1917 2005

HARRIET
1917 1992
LOVING
MOM & DAD

PIERSON
DAVID O
1ST LT USAAF

IMOGENE B
1922 2006
TOGETHER
AGAIN

TREPAK
PETER
SGT USA
VIETNAM
1947 2006

SPERLING
DOROTHY R
MSGT USAF
VIETNAM
1947 2006

HAMMOND
ROBERT L
SP4 USA
1939 2006

GOD BLESS YOU

READ
JOHN H
SSG USA
WWII VIETNAM
1921 2002
SATOKO
1927 2005
YASURAKANI
LOVE ALWAYS
FAMILY

Barrancas National Cemetery, Bushnell, Florida

MICKEY ROONEY

April 2007

D URING WORLD WAR II, I SERVED THREE YEARS AS A PRIVATE IN GENERAL Patton's Third Army. It is an experience I will never forget. I had the great honor to be awarded a bronze star that was presented by General Patton himself. I still wear it proudly today, because it is something my country gave to me.

America is slowly forgetting the value of our veterans and the sacrifice that each and every one of them has made. However, it is not only the veteran, but the whole veteran family that we as Americans must do more to support. Imagine if you would, wives missing their husbands, children missing their fathers or mothers. And not just for a short time, but until their job, the job of keeping our American way of life alive and well, is finished.

GEORGIA NATIONAL CEMETERY, CANTON, GEORGIA

I am a proud member of American Legion Post 43 in Hollywood. Many of my fellow members work in the film and television industry and have also served their country honorably. Veterans are not just soldiers who've landed on beaches or pilots who've had dogfights with the enemy. As important as those roles are, it takes a full cast of people from a broad range of professions, sharing a variety of responsibilities, to make a mighty military force. Everyone—cooks, physicians, supply officers, machinists, radio operators, and logistics specialists—plays a vital part in making the whole operation work smoothly. Each and every soldier has as important a role as the next, and we shouldn't think of one as better than another. Every man and woman who has worn the uniform must be given the same respect that the uniform of the United States of America demands and deserves.

HAMPTON NATIONAL CEMETERY,
HAMPTON, VIRGINIA

My wife Jan and I tour all over the country a great deal. At every performance, we ask all of the veterans in the audience to stand and we applaud them and thank them for their efforts on behalf of our country. Jan then leads the crowd in singing "God Bless America," and there is not a dry eye in the house. It is truly a touching, moving moment during our show to be able to recognize and honor the brave men and women who have given so much of themselves to our country while proudly serving in the U.S. Army, Air Force, Navy, Marines, and Coast Guard. Thank you and God bless each and every one of you!

* * *

"Courage charms us, because it indicates that a man loves an idea better than all things in the world, that he is thinking neither of his bed, nor his dinner, nor his money, but will venture all to put in act the invisible thought of his mind."

—RALPH WALDO EMERSON

FLORIDA NATIONAL CEMETERY, BUSHNELL, FLORIDA

BEAUFORT NATIONAL CEMETERY, BEAUFORT, SOUTH CAROLINA

Houston National Cemetery, Houston, Texas
(Opposite): Hampton National Cemetery, Hampton, Virginia

* * *

"Honor to the soldier, and sailor everywhere, who bravely bears
his country's cause. Honor to him . . . who braves, for the common good,
the storms of Heaven and the storms of battle."

—Abraham Lincoln

VICTOR J.
KOHLBECK
RGINIA

George W. Bush
Excerpt from
Address to the Nation

September 11, 2001

GOOD EVENING. TODAY, OUR FELLOW CITIZENS, OUR WAY OF LIFE, OUR very freedom, came under attack in a series of deliberate and deadly terrorist acts. The victims were in airplanes, or in their offices; secretaries, businessmen and women, military and federal workers; moms and dads, friends and neighbors. Thousands of lives were suddenly ended by evil, despicable acts of terror.

The pictures of airplanes flying into buildings, fires burning, huge structures collapsing, have filled us with disbelief, terrible sadness, and a quiet, unyielding anger. These acts of mass murder were intended to frighten our nation into chaos and retreat. But they have failed; our country is strong.

A great people has been moved to defend a great nation. Terrorist attacks can shake the foundations of our biggest buildings, but they cannot touch the foundation of America. These acts shattered steel, but they cannot dent the steel of American resolve.

America was targeted for attack because we're the brightest beacon for freedom and opportunity in the world. And no one will keep that light from shining.

Today, our nation saw evil, the very worst of human nature. And we responded with the best of America—with the daring of our rescue workers, with the caring for strangers and neighbors who came to give blood and help in any way they could.

(OPPOSITE): MARIETTA NATIONAL CEMETERY, MARIETTA, GEORGIA

Immediately following the first attack, I implemented our government's emergency response plans. Our military is powerful, and it's prepared. Our emergency teams are working in New York City and Washington, D.C., to help with local rescue efforts.

Our first priority is to get help to those who have been injured, and to take every precaution to protect our citizens at home and around the world from further attacks....

The search is under way for those who are behind these evil acts. I've directed the full resources of our intelligence and law enforcement communities to find those responsible and to bring them to justice. We will make no distinction between the terrorists who committed these acts and those who harbor them.

SALISBURY NATIONAL CEMETERY, SALISBURY, NORTH CAROLINA

I appreciate so very much the members of Congress who have joined me in strongly condemning these attacks. And on behalf of the American people, I thank the many world leaders who have called to offer their condolences and assistance.

America and our friends and allies join with all those who want peace and security in the world, and we stand together to win the war against terrorism. Tonight, I ask for your prayers for all those who grieve, for the children whose worlds have been shattered, for all whose sense of safety and security has been threatened. And I pray they will be comforted by a power greater than any of us, spoken through the ages in Psalm 23: "Even though I walk through the valley of the shadow of death, I fear no evil, for You are with me."

This is a day when all Americans from every walk of life unite in our resolve for justice and peace. America has stood down enemies before, and we will do so this time. None of us will ever forget this day. Yet, we go forward to defend freedom and all that is good and just in our world.

Thank you. Good night, and God bless America.

FLORIDA NATIONAL CEMETERY, BUSHNELL, FLORIDA

ARLINGTON NATIONAL CEMETERY, ARLINGTON, VIRGINIA

ETERNAL FATHER, STRONG TO SAVE

* * *

Lord, guard and guide the men who fly

And those who on the ocean ply;

Be with our troops upon the land,

And all who for their country stand:

Be with these guardians day and night

And may their trust be in Thy might.

—*Author Unknown (1955)*

CALVERTON NATIONAL CEMETERY, CALVERTON, NEW YORK

THE NORTHEAST

"...I still remember the refrain of one of the most
popular barracks ballads of that day which proclaimed
most proudly that old soldiers never die;
they just fade away."

—*Douglas MacArthur*

GEORGE WASHINGTON
GENERAL ORDERS

March 1, 1778
Headquarters, Valley Forge

THE COMMANDER IN CHIEF AGAIN TAKES OCCASION TO RETURN HIS warmest thanks to the virtuous officers and soldiery of this army for that persevering fidelity and zeal which they have uniformly manifested in all their conduct. Their fortitude not only under the common hardships incident to a military life but also under the additional sufferings to which the peculiar situation of these states have exposed them, clearly proves them worthy of the enviable privilege of contending for the rights of human nature, the freedom and independence of their country. The recent instance of uncomplaining patience during the scarcity of provisions in camp is a fresh proof that they possess in an eminent degree the spirit of soldiers and the magnanimity of patriots....

Surely we who are free citizens in arms engaged in a struggle for everything valuable in society and partaking in the glorious task of laying the foundation of

(ABOVE): MASSACHUSETTS NATIONAL CEMETERY, BOURNE, MASSACHUSETTS
(OPPOSITE): INDIANTOWN GAP NATIONAL CEMETERY, ANNVILLE, PENNSYLVANIA

an empire, should scorn effeminately to shrink under those accidents and rigours of war which mercenary hirelings fighting in the cause of lawless ambition, rapine and devastation, encounter with cheerfulness and alacrity, we should not be merely equal, we should be superior to them in every qualification that dignifies the man or the soldier in proportion as the motive from which we act and the final hopes of our toils, are superior to theirs.

Thank Heaven! Our country abounds with provision and with prudent management we need not apprehend want for any length of time. Defects in the commissaries department, contingencies of weather, and other temporary impediments have subjected and may again subject us to a deficiency for a few days, but soldiers! American soldiers! Will despise the meanness of repining at such trifling strokes of adversity, trifling indeed when compared to the transcendent prize which will undoubtedly crown their patience and perseverance, glory and freedom, peace and plenty, to themselves and the community; the admiration of the world, the love of their country and the gratitude of posterity!

Bath National Cemetery, Bath, New York

As Long As Someone
Thinks of You and
Remembers You,
You're Not Really Gone.
Jeanine M. Waterman

CALVERTON NATIONAL CEMETERY, CALVERTON, NEW YORK

* * *

"Our debt to the heroic men and valiant women in the service of our country

can never be repaid. They have earned our undying gratitude;

America will never forget their sacrifice."

—HARRY S. TRUMAN

Massachusetts National Cemetery, Bourne, Massachusetts

"They fought together as brothers-in-arms, they died together, and now they sleep side by side. To them we have a solemn obligation."

—CHESTER NIMITZ

CALVERTON NATIONAL CEMETERY, CALVERTON, NEW YORK

* * *

"I was ten years old when World War II ended. I thought the returning veterans

were giants who had saved the world from barbarism. I still think so. I remain a

hero worshipper. Over the decades I've interviewed thousands of the veterans.

It is a privilege to hear their stories, then write them up."

—STEPHEN AMBROSE

CALVERTON NATIONAL CEMETERY, CALVERTON, NEW YORK

Philadelphia National Cemetery, Philadelphia, Pennsylvania

DENNIS MILLER

June 2007

I AM A PERSON WHO BELIEVES THAT GREATNESS IN ALL ENDEAVORS SHOULD BE noted only after the truly great are honored first. Everything we have in America—every belief, every dream, and every freedom, especially in these turbulent times—will only remain intact by relying on the greatness of our armed forces to protect these gifts.

The true hero is the American veteran, who throughout history has been summoned to the altar of selfless courage. I believe we have nothing as a nation without their sacrifice.

I continually remind my sons that, while they admire pro athletes and movie stars, they should reserve their deepest gratitude for the Armed Forces of America.

I thank you from the bottom of my heart for giving America and my family what we have today.

CALVERTON NATIONAL CEMETERY, CALVERTON, NEW YORK

"*Freedom is never more than one*
generation away from extinction.
We didn't pass it to our children in
the bloodstream. It must be fought for,
protected, and handed on for them
to do the same, or one day we will
spend our sunset telling our children
and our children's children what it
was once like in the United States
where men were free."

—RONALD REAGAN

MASSACHUSETTS NATIONAL CEMETERY,
BOURNE, MASSACHUSETTS

58

Long Island National Cemetery, Farmingdale, New York

Laura Ingraham
"The People Supporting the Heroes"

An Excerpt from Power to the People

I WAS TRAVELING HOME FROM COLORADO IN EARLY 2007 AND NOTICED A group of about fifteen World War II veterans gathered at the gate. They had their baseball caps on with their ship names or unit names on them. I struck up a conversation with one who had fought at Iwo Jima and another who was one of the "Band of Brothers." Their escorts, all of whom seemed to be in their twenties and thirties, told me that they were part of the Greatest Generations Foundation. This Denver-based non-profit organization is dedicated to preserving the stories of our war veterans and making it possible for them to travel to the battlefields where they fought. Those vets—many in wheelchairs and using walkers—were going to the World War II Memorial in Washington, D.C. Courtesy of the GGF, many others are traveling to Normandy and the site of the Battle of the Bulge to share "battlefield remembrances." Why not do more to preserve the memory of our real heroes instead of clogging our memories

CALVERTON NATIONAL CEMETERY,
CALVERTON, NEW YORK

with stories about plastic celebrities? Why not celebrate the veterans in our own families? Why not make sure our kids can tell the difference between a real hero—the one with medals on his chest—from a pop idol?

INDIANTOWN GAP NATIONAL CEMETERY, ANNVILLE, PENNSYLVANIA

* * *

"In the truest sense, freedom cannot be bestowed; it must be achieved."

—FRANKLIN D. ROOSEVELT

Paul Teutul, Sr.

May 2007

AMERICA IS MORE THAN A COUNTRY; IT'S A SPIRIT — A DREAM THAT LIVES IN each of us. There is no other place on earth like it. America really is the land of opportunity and freedom—freedom to choose our career, our faith, our lives. This dream, the American dream, has always been and continues to be kept alive by the men and women of our military who stand up and defend it.

I know about the American dream because I'm living it. I started out building custom choppers in the basement of my home in Montgomery, NY, and have made a living doing what I love ever since. The pride my sons and I have in this country and in our military heroes is reflected in a lot of the choppers we've crafted over the years. The first bike that we built for our show, *American Chopper*, was the Jet bike to honor our military. We unveiled the Jet bike aboard the USS *Intrepid* in New York City. For another episode we built two bikes that were auctioned, also aboard the *Intrepid*, with the proceeds going to charities that support the military, like the Fischer House Foundation and the Fallen Heroes Fund. We are also very proud of the POW-MIA bike we built in honor of our veterans and the Comanche bike built in honor of the army. We continue to use our success to find creative ways to support our troops and their families.

We realize the debt we owe to the courageous and honorable people of our armed services who do the hardest jobs for the greatest cause. It is their blood and sweat, their fearlessness, and their fierce loyalty to freedom that lets the rest of us be free to live our dreams. My sons and I build bikes in their honor to thank them the best we know how for being the bravest, greatest military in the world.

God bless America.

(OPPOSITE): MASSACHUSETTS NATIONAL CEMETERY, BOURNE, MASSACHUSETTS

Calverton National Cemetery, Calverton, New York

BEVERLY NATIONAL CEMETERY, BEVERLY, NEW JERSEY

✳   ✳   ✳

"Patriotism is not short, frenzied outbursts of emotion,
but the tranquil and steady dedication of a lifetime."

—ADLAI E. STEVENSON

Massachusetts National Cemetery, Bourne, Massachusetts

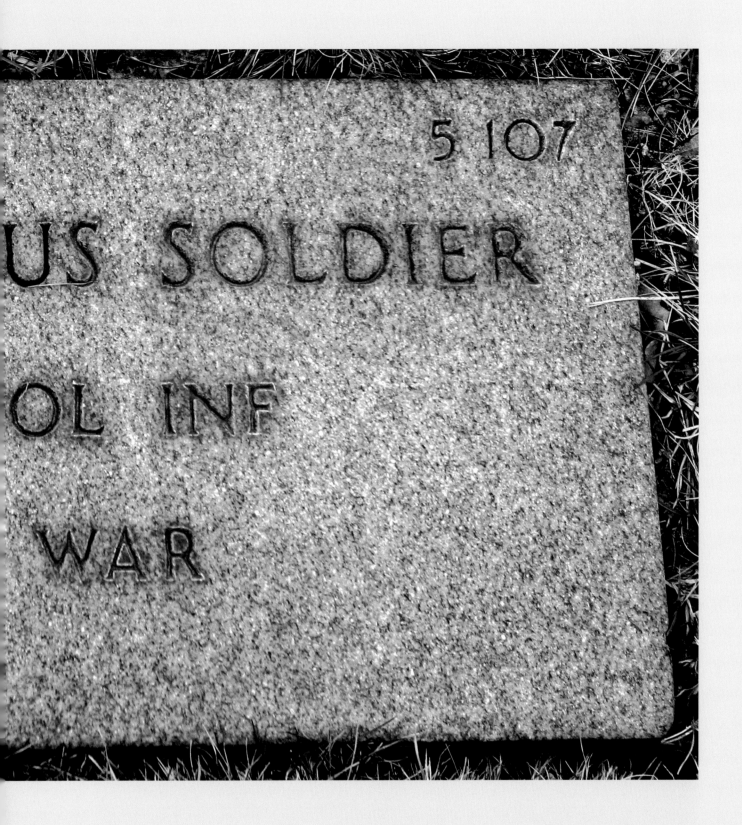

"We come, not to mourn our dead soldiers, but to praise them."

—Francis A. Walker

Philadelphia National Cemetery, Philadelphia, Pennsylvania

WOODROW WILSON
EXCERPT FROM
ADDRESS TO CONGRESS

April 2, 1917

WE ARE GLAD, NOW THAT WE SEE THE FACTS WITH NO VEIL OF FALSE pretense about them, to fight thus for the ultimate peace of the world and for the liberation of its peoples, the German peoples included: for the rights of nations great and small and the privilege of men everywhere to choose their way of life and of obedience. The world must be made safe for democracy. Its peace must be planted upon the tested foundations of political liberty. We have no selfish ends to serve ....

TOGUS NATIONAL CEMETERY, TOGUS, MAINE

It is a distressing and oppressive duty, gentlemen of the Congress, which I have performed in thus addressing you. There are, it may be, many months of fiery trial and sacrifice ahead of us. It is a fearful thing to lead this great peaceful people into war, into the most terrible and disastrous of all wars, civilization itself seeming to be in the balance.

But the right is more precious than peace, and we shall fight for the things which we have always carried nearest our hearts, for democracy, for the right of those who submit to authority to have a voice in their own governments, for the rights and liberties of small nations, for a universal dominion of right by such a concert of free peoples as shall bring peace and safety to all nations and make the world at last free.

FINNS POINT NATIONAL CEMETERY,
SALEM, NEW JERSEY

To such a task we can dedicate our lives and our fortunes, everything that we are and everything that we have, with the pride of those who know that the day has come when America is privileged to spend her blood and her might for the principles that gave her birth and happiness and the peace which she has treasured. God helping her, she can do no other.

☆　☆　☆

"Are they dead that yet speak louder than we can speak, and a more universal language? Are they dead that yet act? Are they dead that yet move upon society and inspire the people with nobler motives and more heroic patriotism?"

—HENRY WARD BEECHER

WOODLAWN NATIONAL CEMETERY, ELMIRA, NEW YORK

CALVERTON NATIONAL CEMETERY, CALVERTON, NEW YORK

THE HISTORY OF "TAPS"

AN EXCERPT FROM

Twenty-Four Notes That Tap Deep Emotions:
The Story of America's Most Famous Bugle Call

by Jari Villanueva

O F ALL THE MILITARY BUGLE CALLS, NONE IS SO EASILY RECOGNIZED OR more apt to render emotion than the call "Taps." The melody is both eloquent and haunting and the history of its origin is interesting and somewhat clouded in controversy. In the British Army, a similar type call known as "Last Post" has been sounded over soldiers' graves since 1885, but the use of "Taps" is unique to the United States military, since the call is sounded at funerals, wreath-laying, and memorial services.

"Taps" began as a revision to the signal for Extinguish Lights (Lights Out) at the end of the day. Up until the Civil War, the infantry call for Extinguish Lights was the one set down in Silas Casey's (1801–1882) "Tactics," which had been borrowed from the French. The music for "Taps" was adapted by Union General Daniel Butterfield for his brigade (Third Brigade, First Division, Fifth Army Corps, Army of the Potomac) in July 1862.

As the story goes, General Butterfield was not pleased with the call for Extinguish Lights, feeling that the call was too formal to signal the day's end, and with the help

MASSACHUSETTS NATIONAL CEMETERY, BOURNE, MASSACHUSETTS

of the brigade bugler, Oliver Willcox Norton (1839–1920), wrote "Taps" to honor his men while in camp at Harrison's Landing, Virginia, following the Seven Days battle. These battles took place during the Peninsular Campaign of 1862. The new call, sounded that night in July 1862, soon spread to other units of the Union Army and was reportedly also used by the Confederates. "Taps" was made an official bugle call after the war.

In the interest of historical accuracy, it should be noted that General Butterfield did not compose "Taps," rather that he revised an earlier call into the present day bugle call we know as "Taps." This is not meant to take credit away from him.

How did the call become associated with funerals? The earliest official reference to the mandatory use of "Taps" at military funeral ceremonies is found in the U.S. Army Infantry Drill Regulations for 1891, although it had doubtless been used unofficially long before that time, under its former designation Extinguish Lights. The first sounding of "Taps" at a military funeral is commemorated in a stained glass window at the Chapel of the Centurion (the Old Post Chapel) at Fort Monroe, Virginia.

The site where "Taps" was born is also commemorated by a monument located on the grounds of Berkeley Plantation, Virginia. This monument to "Taps" was erected by the Virginia American Legion and dedicated on July 4, 1969. The site is also rich in history, for the Harrisons of Berkeley Plantation included Benjamin Harrison and William Henry Harrison, both presidents of the United States as well as Benjamin Harrison (father and great grandfather of future presidents), a signer of the Declaration of Independence.

Why the name "Taps"? The call of Tattoo was used in order to assemble soldiers for the last roll call of the day. Tattoo may have originated during the Thirty Years' War (1618–1648) or during the wars of King William III during the 1690s. The word tattoo in this usage is derived from the Dutch tap (tap or faucet) and toe (to cut off). When it was time to cease drinking for the evening and return to the post, the provost or Officer of the Day, accompanied by a sergeant and drummer, would go through the town beating out the signal. As far as military regulations went, there was a prescribed roll call to be taken "at Taptoe time" to ensure that all the troops had returned to their billets. It is possible that the word Tattoo became "Taps." Tattoo was also called "Tap-toe" and as is true with slang terms in the military, it was shortened to "Taps." The other, and more likely, explanation is that the name "Taps" was borrowed from a drummer's beat. The beating of Tattoo by the drum corps would be followed by the Drummer of the Guard beating three distinct drum taps at four count intervals for the military evolution Extinguish Lights. During the American Civil War, Extinguish Lights was the bugle call used as the final call of the day and as the name implies, it was a signal to extinguish all fires and lights.

Following the call, three single drum strokes were beat at four-count intervals. This was known as the "Drum Taps" or in common usage of soldiers "The Taps" or "Taps." There are many references to the term "Taps" before the war and during the conflict, before the bugle call we are all familiar with came into existence. So the drum beat that followed Extinguish Lights came to be called "Taps" by the common soldiers and when the new bugle call was created in July 1862 to replace the more formal sounding Extinguish Lights, (the one Butterfield disliked), the bugle call also came to be known as "Taps." The new bugle signal (also known as "Butterfield's Lullaby") is called "Taps" in common usage because it is used for the same purpose as the three drum taps. However the U.S. Army still called it Extinguish Lights and it did not officially change the name to "Taps" until 1891.

As soon as "Taps" was sounded that night in July 1862, words were put with the music. The first were, "Go To Sleep, Go to Sleep." As the years went on many more versions were created. There are no official words to the music but here are some of the more popular verses:

Day is done, gone the sun,
From the hills, from the lake,
From the sky.
All is well, safely rest,
God is nigh.

Fades the light; And afar
Goeth day, And the stars
Shineth bright,
Fare thee well; Day has gone,
Night is on.

Thanks and praise, For our days,
'Neath the sun, 'Neath the stars,
'Neath the sky,
As we go, This we know,
God is nigh.

As with many other customs, this solemn tradition continues today. Although Butterfield merely revised an earlier bugle call, his role in producing those twenty-four notes gives him a place in the history of music as well as the history of war.

Philadelphia National Cemetery, Philadelphia, Pennsylvania

Long Island National Cemetery, Farmingdale, New York

Calverton National Cemetery, Calverton, New York

ROSUCK
JACK E
PFC USA

ELLEN
1928   2002
TOGETHER

OLIVER WENDELL HOLMES, JR.

Excerpt from Memorial Day Address
May 30, 1884

NOT LONG AGO, I HEARD A YOUNG MAN ASK WHY PEOPLE STILL KEEP UP Memorial Day, and it set me thinking of the answer. Not the answer that you and I should give to each other—not the expression of those feelings that, so long as you and I live, will make this day sacred to memories of love and grief and heroic youth—but an answer which should command the assent of those who do not share our memories, and in which we of the North and our brethren of the South could join in perfect accord.

ANNAPOLIS NATIONAL CEMETERY, ANNAPOLIS, MARYLAND

...So to the indifferent inquirer who asks why Memorial Day is still kept up we may answer: It celebrates and solemnly reaffirms from year to year a national act of enthusiasm and faith. It embodies in the most impressive form our belief that to act with enthusiasm and faith is the condition of acting greatly. To fight out a war, you must believe in something and want something with all your might. So must you do to carry anything else to an end worth reaching. More than that, you must be willing to commit yourself to a course, perhaps a long and hard one, without being able to foresee exactly where you will come out. All that is required of you is that you should go somewhither as hard as ever you can. The rest belongs to fate. One may fall—at the beginning of the charge or at the top of the earthworks—but in no other way can he reach the rewards of victory.

. . . Year after year, the comrades of the dead follow with public honor, procession and commemorative flags, and funeral march—honor and grief from us who stand almost alone. . . . But grief is not the end of all. I seem to hear the funeral march become a paean. I see beyond the forest the moving banners of a hidden column. Our dead brothers still live for us, and bid us think of life, not death—of life to which in their youth they lent the passion and glory of the spring. As I listen, the great chorus of life and joy begins again, and amid the awful orchestra of seen and unseen powers and destinies of good and evil our trumpets sound once more a note of daring, hope, and will.

GERALD B.H. SOLOMON SARATOGA NATIONAL CEMETERY, SCHUYLERVILLE, NEW YORK
(OPPOSITE): INDIANTOWN GAP NATIONAL CEMETERY, ANNVILLE, PENNSYLVANIA

*   *   *

"Sure I wave the American flag. Do you know
a better flag to wave? Sure I love my country
with all her faults. I'm not ashamed of that.
Never have been, never will be."

—JOHN WAYNE

Calverton National Cemetery, Calverton, New York

Eternal Father, Strong to Save

* * *

Eternal Father, grant, we pray,

To all Marines, both night and day,

The courage, honor, strength, and skill

Their land to serve, thy law fulfill

Be thou the shield forevermore

From every peril to the Corps.

—J. E. Seim (1966)

To the
Memory of
175
Non Com.
OFFICERS
and Privates
of the
56. U.S.C. Infty.

Died of Cholera in
August 1866.

Jefferson Barracks National Cemetery, St. Louis, Missouri

The Midwest

"My religious belief teaches me to feel as safe in battle as in bed.
God has fixed the time for my death. I do not concern myself
about that, but to be always ready, no matter when it may
overtake me. That is the way all men should live,
and then all would be equally brave."

—*Thomas "Stonewall" Jackson*

FORT CUSTER NATIONAL CEMETERY, AUGUSTA, MICHIGAN

＊　＊　＊

"Sleep, soldiers!
Still in honored rest
Your truth and valor wearing:
The bravest are the tenderest,
The loving are the daring."

—BAYARD TAYLOR

Dayton National Cemetery, Dayton, Ohio

* * *

"My God! How little do my countrymen know what precious blessings

they are in possession of, and which no other people on earth enjoy!"

—Thomas Jefferson

Abraham Lincoln
Gettysburg Address

November 19, 1863
Gettysburg, Pennsylvania

FOUR SCORE AND SEVEN YEARS AGO, OUR FATHERS BROUGHT FORTH ON THIS continent a new nation, conceived in liberty and dedicated to the proposition that all men are created equal.

Now we are engaged in a great civil war, testing whether that nation or any nation so conceived and so dedicated can long endure. We are met on a great battlefield of that war. We have come to dedicate a portion of that field as a final resting place for those who here gave their lives that that nation might live. It is altogether fitting and proper that we should do this.

But, in a larger sense, we cannot dedicate, we cannot consecrate, we cannot hallow this ground. The brave men, living and dead who struggled here, have consecrated it far above our poor power to add or detract. The world will little note nor long remember what we say here, but it can never forget what they did here. It is for us the living rather to be dedicated here to the unfinished work which they who fought here have thus far so nobly advanced. It is rather for us to be here dedicated to the great task remaining before us—that from these honored dead we take increased devotion to that cause for which they gave the last full measure of devotion—that we here highly resolve that these dead shall not have died in vain, that this nation under God shall have a new birth of freedom, and that government of the people, by the people, for the people shall not perish from the earth.

Jefferson Barracks National Cemetery, St. Louis, Missouri

Fort McPherson National Cemetery,
Maxwell, Nebraska

Ohio Western Reserve National Cemetery,
Rittman, Ohio

Fort Custer National Cemetery, Augusta, Michigan

OLIVER NORTH
THE SOLDIER, THE SILENCE, AND THE SOD

T HEY ARE PEOPLE, PLACES AND RITUALS SEARED INTO MY MEMORY: MEN AND women I have known—in the best and worst of times; cemeteries, all remarkably alike and yet each so different; and tender graveside ceremonies for those who have served our nation. More times than I can count, I have stood at the memorial of a fallen friend who was mourned by family and loved ones, honored by his country, and laid to rest with fellow warriors who are eternally retired from the burdens of war.

Our tears fall gently on the sod where soldiers sleep, while our hearts cry for a life taken too soon. This is sacred soil, consecrated by the sacrifices of those who served as our nation's uniformed guardians. At their memorial services, it matters not whether there is a warm sun or a bitter cold, the silence is what I remember most.

Every warrior prays for the blessings of a serene silence, but is cursed by a quiet battlefield. On a jungle patrol, tranquility can be pierced by the snap of a twig or the

ABRAHAM LINCOLN NATIONAL CEMETERY, ELWOOD, ILLINOIS

shot of a sniper. A hushed desert wind provides no comfort to those caught by the explosion of a roadside bomb. In combat, silence is fragile terrain for the warrior to navigate because it is so easily wrecked by an enemy.

When the quiet is broken, unleashed is the unforgettable, unforgivable, clamor of war. Shattered silence brings the vicious cadence of machine gun fire; the indiscriminate blast of a grenade or mortar round; the unmistakable thud of a human body falling to the ground; the indescribable cries of pain from a soldier, sailor, airman, Guardsman or Marine whose flesh has been ripped open by flying shrapnel; the last gasp of breath of a dying friend.

But on the hallowed grounds of our national cemeteries, these sounds are heard no more. The distant dirge of the pipes, the faint call of a bugle, and the crisp snap of a flag in the wind are the only sounds which dare to invade the peace of warriors at rest.

"Only the dead have seen the end of war," Plato said. My solace is in the words of my Savior to the Apostle John: "Father I will that those you have given me, be with me where I am."

We mourn their loss and then entrust these selfless Americans to our national cemeteries where they rest beneath a white marble stone. Visit them, but tread lightly near each hero's grave. Pray for them and their families, but do so quietly, for during their lives they had to endure the horrific sounds of war. And be grateful that here, in honored respite, these fallen champions can embrace what every warrior hopes for—a peaceful silence.

⋆ ⋆ ⋆

"The liberties of our country, the freedom of our civil constitution, are worth defending against all hazards; and it is our duty to defend them against all attacks."

—SAMUEL ADAMS

Dayton National Cemetery, Dayton, Ohio

* * *

"The solder, above all other people, prays for peace,

for he must suffer and bear the deepest wounds."

—Douglas MacArthur

Dayton National Cemetery, Dayton, Ohio

FRED TRAVALENA

April 2007

THE WIND AND THE GRASS INTERTWINE, MAKING A CARPET AROUND THE hallowed ground of the United States servicemen and women laid to rest in military cemeteries all over the world. These were Americans who made the ultimate sacrifice for all of us who live in freedom.

Sacred Grounds that are scattered across the four corners of the earth because of the list of battles from Iwo Jima, Normandy, Salerno, North Korea, Vietnam, Persian Gulf, the Ardennes, Baghdad, Afghanistan, and Gettysburg.

So young, so brave, in spite of their fears, in spite of what they witnessed, the horrors of war and its toll on human life…they fought on to victory.

The year before my dad died we had an occasion to go for a walk after dinner. He knew he was ill but chose to not tell us. As we walked, Dad became somber. He said, "Fred, I wish I had been a bigger success so I could leave you something when I go."

JEFFERSON BARRACKS NATIONAL CEMETERY, ST. LOUIS, MISSOURI

I told him that he and Mom gave me life and talent. Legacy and material things were not important to me. Look at my beautiful home and family. "Besides, Dad, you have done a lot of great things in your life and career." Dad said, "Thanks, but there is only one thing of which I am truly proud. My service in the United States Army in World War II during the Battle of the Bulge." Dad received two Purple Hearts and a Silver Star Citation. He is buried at Calverton Veterans Cemetery in Patchoque, New York.

OHIO WESTERN RESERVE NATIONAL CEMETERY,
RITTMAN, OHIO

On November 8, 1992, this writer produced The National Reconciliation Day ceremonies in Washington, D.C., and the walk to Arlington Cemetery where dignitaries and celebrities came together with music, speeches, and testimony to reconcile and forgive.

An old soldier who attended the ceremonies asked me if I was Fred Travalena's son. He said he went through the war with my dad and that they shared many foxholes together: "He was one tough little guy." He then stood on stage with all of us for the ceremony of Reconciliation and Forgiveness.

✫　✫　✫

Greater love hath no man
Then that he lay down his life
For another….
Walk humbly on these Sacred Grounds

KEOKUK NATIONAL CEMETERY, KEOKUK, IOWA

✳ ✳ ✳

"Men acquainted with the battlefield will not be found among

the numbers that glibly talk of another way."

—DWIGHT D. EISENHOWER

Ohio Western Reserve National Cemetery, Rittman, Ohio

ETERNAL FATHER,
STRONG TO SAVE

* * *

Eternal Father, strong to save,

Whose arm hath bound the restless wave,

Who bidd'st the mighty ocean deep

Its own appointed limits keep;

Oh, hear us when we cry to Thee,

For those in peril on the sea!

—*William Whiting (1860)*

Fort Custer National Cemetery, Augusta, Michigan

Jefferson Barracks National Cemetery,
St. Louis, Missouri

* * *

*"They are dead; but they live in each Patriot's breast,
and their names are engraven on honor's bright crest."*

—Henry Wadsworth Longfellow

Jefferson Barracks National Cemetery,
St. Louis, Missouri

FRANKLIN D. ROOSEVELT
EXCERPT FROM ADDRESS TO CONGRESS

December 8, 1941

MR. VICE PRESIDENT, AND MR. SPEAKER, AND MEMBERS OF THE SENATE and the House of Representatives:

Yesterday, December 7, 1941—a date which will live in infamy—the United States of America was suddenly and deliberately attacked by naval and air forces of the Empire of Japan.

…Japan has, therefore, undertaken a surprise offensive extending throughout the Pacific area. The facts of yesterday and today speak for themselves. The people of the United States have already formed their opinions and well understand the implications to the very life and safety of our nation.

As commander in chief of the army and navy, I have directed that all measures be taken for our defense.

But always will our whole nation remember the character of the onslaught against us.

No matter how long it may take us to overcome this premeditated invasion, the American people in their righteous might will win through to absolute victory.

…With confidence in our armed forces—with the unbounding determination of our people—we will gain the inevitable triumph—so help us God.

(OPPOSITE): FORT CUSTER NATIONAL CEMETERY, AUGUSTA, MICHIGAN

Jefferson Barracks National Cemetery, St. Louis, Missouri

Dayton National Cemetery, Dayton, Ohio

FORT CUSTER NATIONAL CEMETERY, AUGUSTA, MICHIGAN

"This nation will remain the land
of the free only so long as it is the
home of the brave."

—ELMER DAVIS

ANDREW P
TITUS JR
LT COL
US ARMY
WORLD WAR II
KOREA
NOV 21 1913

FORT CUSTER NATIONAL CEMETERY, AUGUSTA, MICHIGAN

JEFFERSON BARRACKS NATIONAL CEMETERY, ST. LOUIS, MISSOURI

* * *

"Over the years, the United States has sent many of its fine young men and women

into great peril to fight for freedom beyond our borders. The only amount of land

we have ever asked for in return is enough to bury those that did not return . . . ."

—COLIN POWELL

Dwight D. Eisenhower
Address to the
Allied Expeditionary Forces

June 6, 1944
England

Soldiers, sailors, and airmen of the Allied Expeditionary Forces: You are about to embark upon the Great Crusade, toward which we have striven these many months. The eyes of the world are upon you. The hopes and prayers of liberty-loving people everywhere march with you. In company with our brave Allies and brothers-in-arms on other fronts you will bring about the destruction of the German war machine, the elimination of Nazi tyranny over oppressed peoples of Europe, and security for ourselves in a free world.

Your task will not be an easy one. Your enemy is well trained, well equipped, and battle hardened. He will fight savagely.

But this is the year 1944! Much has happened since the Nazi triumphs of 1940–41. The United Nations have inflicted upon the Germans great defeats, in open battle, man-to-man. Our air offensive has seriously reduced their strength in the air and their capacity to wage war on the ground. Our home fronts have given us an overwhelming superiority in weapons and munitions of war, and placed at our disposal great reserves of trained fighting men. The tide has turned! The free men of the world are marching together to victory!

I have full confidence in your courage, devotion to duty, and skill in battle. We will accept nothing less than full victory!

Good luck! And let us all beseech the blessings of Almighty God upon this great and noble undertaking.

OHIO WESTERN RESERVE NATIONAL CEMETERY, RITTMAN, OHIO

* * *

"I have never been able to think of the day as one of mourning; I have never quite been able to feel

that half-masted flags were appropriate on Decoration Day. I have rather felt that the flag should be

at the peak, because those whose dying we commemorate rejoiced in seeing it where their valor

placed it. We honor them in a joyous, thankful, trimphant commemoration of what they did."

—BENJAMIN HARRISON

JEFFERSON BARRACKS NATIONAL CEMETERY, ST. LOUIS, MISSOURI

Joshua Lawrence Chamberlain
Excerpt from the Dedication
of the Maine Monument

October 3, 1889
Gettysburg, Pennsylvania

A QUARTER OF A CENTURY AGO ON THIS RUGGED CREST YOU WERE DOING what you deemed your duty. Today you come with modest mien, with care more for truth than for praise, to retrace and record the simple facts—the outward form—of your movements and actions. But far more than this entered into your thought and motive, and far greater was the result of the action taken than any statistical description of it could import.

You were making history; the world has recorded for you more than you have written. The centuries to come will share and recognize the victory won here, with growing gratitude. The country has acknowledged your service. Your state is proud of it.

GREAT LAKES NATIONAL CEMETERY, HOLLY, MICHIGAN

This well-earned and unsought fame has moved you already to acknowledge your deserts. Your own loyal and loving zeal for justice has indeed anticipated the state's recognition. At your own cost you set your monument here to mark the ground where faithful service and devotion wrought a result so momentous . . . .

I could see all this on your faces when you were coming into position here for the desperate encounter; man by man, file by file, on the right into the line. I knew that you all knew what was staked on your endurance and heroism. Some of you heard Vincent say to me, with such earnest and prophetic eyes, pointing to the right of our position and the front of the oncoming attack, "You understand, Colonel, this ground must be held at all costs!" I did understand; with a heavy weight on my mind and spirit. You understood; and it was done. Held, and at what cost! Held, and for what effect!

We know not of the future, and cannot plan for it much. But we can hold our spirits and our bodies so pure and high, we may cherish such thoughts and such ideals, and dream such dreams of lofty purpose, that we can determine and know what manner of men we will be whenever and wherever the hour strikes, that calls to noble action, this predestination God has given us in charge. No man becomes suddenly different from his habit and cherished thought. We carry our accustomed manners with us. And it was the boyhood you brought from your homes which made you men; which braced your hearts, which shone upon your foreheads, which held you steadfast in mind and body, and lifted these heights of Gettysburg to immortal glory.

Fort Custer National Cemetery,
Augusta, Michigan

Dayton National Cemetery, Dayton, Ohio

New Albany National Cemetery, New Albany, Indiana

Dayton National Cemetery, Dayton, Ohio

ETERNAL FATHER, STRONG TO SAVE

* * *

Lord, guard and guide the men who fly

Through the great spaces in the sky.

Be with them always in the air,

In darkening storms or sunlight fair;

Oh, hear us when we lift our prayer,

For those in peril in the air!

—Mary C. D. Hamilton (1915)

TAHOMA NATIONAL CEMETERY, KENT, WASHINGTON

THE WEST

"This is the great reward of service. To live, far out and on, in the life of others; this is the mystery of the Christ—to give life's best for such high sake that it shall be found again unto life eternal."

—*Joshua Lawrence Chamberlain*

Fort Rosecrans National Cemetery, San Diego, California

Los Angeles National Cemetery, Los Angeles, California

Ronald Reagan
Remarks on the Fortieth Anniversary of D-Day

June 6, 1984
Pointe du Hoc, Normandy, France

We're here to mark that day in history when the Allied armies joined in battle to reclaim this continent to liberty. For four long years, much of Europe had been under a terrible shadow. Free nations had fallen, Jews cried out in the camps, millions cried out for liberation. Europe was enslaved and the world prayed for its rescue. Here, in Normandy, the rescue began. Here, the Allies stood and fought against tyranny....

The Rangers looked up and saw the enemy soldiers at the edge of the cliffs, shooting down at them with machine guns and throwing grenades. And the American Rangers began to climb. They shot rope ladders over the face of these cliffs and began to pull themselves up. When one Ranger fell, another would take his place. When one rope was cut, a Ranger would grab another and begin his climb again. They climbed, shot back, and held their footing. Soon, one by one, the Rangers pulled themselves over the top, and in seizing the firm land at the top of these cliffs, they began to seize back the continent of Europe. Two hundred and twenty-five came here. After two days of fighting, only ninety could still bear arms.

And behind me is a memorial that symbolizes the Ranger daggers that were thrust into the top of these cliffs. And before me are the men who put them there. These are the boys of Pointe du Hoc. These are the men who took the cliffs. These are the champions who helped free a continent. And these are the heroes who helped end a war. Gentlemen, I look at you and I think of the words of Stephen Spender's poem.

You are men who in your "lives fought for life and left the vivid air signed with your honor."

…The Americans who fought here that morning knew word of the invasion was spreading through the darkness back home. They…felt in their hearts, though they couldn't know in fact, that in Georgia they were filling the churches at 4:00 am. In Kansas they were kneeling on their porches and praying. And in Philadelphia they were ringing the Liberty Bell.

NATIONAL MEMORIAL CEMETERY OF THE PACIFIC,
HONOLULU, HAWAII

Something else helped the men of D-Day; their rock-hard belief that Providence would have a great hand in the events that would unfold here; that God was an ally in this great cause. And so, the night before the invasion, when Colonel Wolverton asked his parachute troops to kneel with him in prayer, he told them: "Do not bow your heads, but look up so you can see God and ask His blessing in what we're about to do." Also, that night, General Matthew Ridgway [was] on his cot, listening in the darkness for the promise God made to Joshua: "I will not fail thee nor forsake thee."

…Here, in this place where the West held together, let us make a vow to our dead. Let us show them by our actions that we understand what they died for. Let our actions say to them the words for which Matthew Ridgway listened: "I will not fail thee nor forsake thee."

Strengthened by their courage and heartened by their valor and borne by their memory, let us continue to stand for the ideals for which they lived and died.

✳ ✳ ✳

"I have returned many times to honor the valiant men who died...

every man who set foot on Omaha Beach was a hero."

—Omar Bradley

National Memorial Cemetery of Arizona, Phoenix, Arizona

FORT LOGAN NATIONAL CEMETERY, DENVER, COLORADO

NATIONAL MEMORIAL CEMETERY OF THE PACIFIC, HONOLULU, HAWAII
(PREVIOUS SPREAD): SAN FRANCISCO NATIONAL CEMETERY, SAN FRANCISCO, CALIFORNIA

＊　＊　＊

"From time to time, the tree of liberty must be watered

with the blood of tyrants and patriots."

—THOMAS JEFFERSON

Ann-Margret
Speech Welcoming Home
Returning American Troops

Nellis Air Force Base, Nevada
November 2005

WELCOME HOME, YOU GUYS. I AM SO EXCITED TO BE HERE. IN JULY OF this year, I was honored to be a part of Operation Homecoming for Vietnam veterans in Branson, Missouri. Today, again, I am thrilled and honored to be here and welcome you home. You all represent the America that I love and cherish.

I did my first USO show when I was a freshman at Northwestern University. We went to Iceland and Germany. In 1966 and 1969 I went to Vietnam to perform and to entertain—but I received so much more than I could ever give. I was very young

NATIONAL MEMORIAL CEMETERY OF ARIZONA, PHOENIX, ARIZONA
(OPPOSITE): FORT LOGAN NATIONAL CEMETERY, DENVER, COLORADO

and I looked at you young men and women and you inspired me with your courage, your bravery, your youth, your lives, your love of country and each other. I can never put into words what it was like looking out from a makeshift stage and seeing the faces from small towns, from large cities—boys—many of them not yet men—but doing a man's job.

You were constantly facing the unknown yet never hesitating, never backing off, but moving forward—such courage, such strength, such heroism—from one group to another. And I remember the applause—and the laughter—the moments of joy.... And then we would leave, and you once again faced another day and night of danger. And there were other heroes too.

San Francicso National Cemetery,
San Francisco, California

All of the wives, husbands, parents, children, brothers, and sisters who were left behind and waited back home for your safe return. I hold these memories near and dear. I realize that I learned so much from that experience going to Vietnam, and although I was never very good at geography, I can still recall places that I went to: Da Nang, Chu Lai, Phu Bai, Cam Rahn Bay, Bien Hoa, Cu Chi, Play Cu, Quant Tri, the *Kitty Hawk*, the *Yorktown* ....

You veterans represent what America is all about: hope, family, unity, grace, and love. I want you all to know you have my respect, my admiration, and my loyalty.

Thank the Good Lord that you all are back here out of harm's way, in the United States of America.

God bless you and welcome home!

National Memorial Cemetery of the Pacific, Honolulu, Hawaii

Tahoma National Cemetery, Kent, Washington

NATIONAL MEMORIAL CEMETERY OF ARIZONA, PHOENIX, ARIZONA

Eagle Point National Cemetery, Eagle Point, Oregon

FORT LOGAN NATIONAL CEMETERY, DENVER, COLORADO

IN MEMORY OF THE MEN WHO
OFFERED THEIR LIVES IN DEFENSE
OF THEIR COUNTRY

George S. Patton
Excerpt from Speech
To the Third Army

Spring 1944
England

ALL REAL AMERICANS LOVE THE STING AND CLASH OF BATTLE. WHEN YOU were kids, you all admired the champion marble player; the fastest runner; the big league ball players; the toughest boxers….Americans play to win—all the time….Death must not be feared….The real hero is the man who fights even though he is scared….Real heroes are not storybook combat fighters, either. Every man in the army plays a vital part. Every little job is essential….Every man is a link in the great chain.

One of the bravest men I ever saw in the African campaign was the fellow I saw on top of a telegraph pole in the midst of furious fire while we were plowing toward Tunis. I stopped and asked him what the hell he was doing up there at that time. He answered, "Fixing the wire, sir." "Isn't it a little unhealthy right now?" I asked. "Yes, sir, but this…wire's got to be fixed." There was a real soldier. There was a man who

GOLDEN GATE NATIONAL CEMETERY,
SAN BRUNO, CALIFORNIA

devoted all he had to his duty, no matter how great the odds….

We'll win this war but we'll win it only by fighting and by showing the Germans we've got more guts than they have….

(OPPOSITE): LOS ANGELES NATIONAL CEMETERY, LOS ANGELES, CALIFORNIA

8 509

GLADYS T
MCNALLY
HIS WIFE
DEC. 23 1918
FEB 12 2001
ALWAYS LOVING
ALWAYS LOVED

Tahoma National Cemetery, Kent, Washington

* * *

"How important it is for us to recognize and celebrate our heroes and she-roes!"

—Maya Angelou

Fort Logan National Cemetery, Denver, Colorado

"Where liberty dwells,
there is my country."

—Benjamin Franklin

PETERSEN
LYLE M
PVT USA
32   2004

KRIVDO
JACK KENNETH
RMI USN
WW II KOREA
1922   2004

TOGETHER
FOREVER

ENK
HOWARD

PUR

LAND
OAN S
C USAF
OREA
2004

MOTHER
DMOT

KARDOS
VID S
USA
NAM

Andrew Jackson
Excerpt from
"Volunteers to Arms" Speech

March 1812

Citizens! Your government has at last yielded to the impulse of the nation….The eternal enemies of American prosperity are again to be taught to respect your rights, after having been compelled to feel, once more, the power of your arms….

A simple invitation is given to the young men of the country to arm for their own and their country's rights. On this invitation 50,000 volunteers, full of martial ardor, indignant at their country's wrongs and burning with impatience to illustrate their names by some signal exploit, are expected to repair the national standard.

…Who are we? And for what are we going to fight? Are we the titled slaves of George the Third? The military conscripts of Napoleon the Great? Or sons of America: the citizens of the only republic existing in the world; and the only people on earth who possess rights, liberties, and property which they dare call their own.

Fort Logan National Cemetery, Denver, Colorado

National Memorial Cemetery of the Pacific, Honolulu, Hawaii
(Opposite): Fort Logan National Cemetery, Denver, Colorado

* * *

"For love of country they accepted death."

—James A. Garfield

National Memorial Cemetery of the Pacific, Honolulu, Hawaii

National Memorial Cemetery of Arizona, Phoenix, Arizona

* * *

"Let every nation know, whether it wishes us well or ill, that we shall pay any price,

bear any burden, meet any hardship, support any friend, oppose any foe,

in order to assure the survival and the success of liberty."

—John F. Kennedy

Los Angeles National Cemetery, Los Angeles, California

National Memorial Cemetery of the Pacific, Honolulu, Hawaii

Bob Hope

I WAS THERE. I SAW YOUR SONS AND YOUR HUSBANDS, YOUR BROTHERS AND your sweethearts. I saw how they worked, played, fought, and lived. I saw some of them die. I saw more courage, more good humor in the face of discomfort, more love in an era of hate, and more devotion to duty than could exist under tyranny.

—On returning from a South Pacific Tour, 1944

* * *

I've been given many awards in my lifetime—but to be numbered among the men and women I admire most is the greatest honor I have ever received.

—On an act of Congress signed by President Bill Clinton
naming Bob Hope an Honorary Veteran, 1997

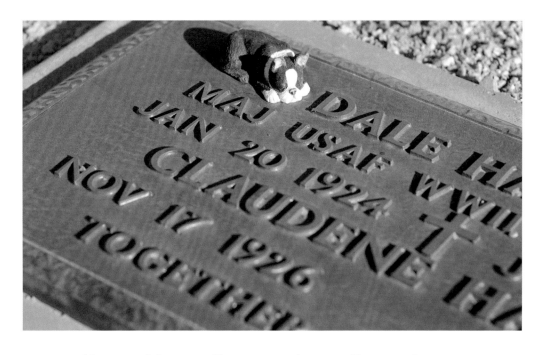

NATIONAL MEMORIAL CEMETERY OF ARIZONA, PHOENIX, ARIZONA

"Time will not dim the
glory of their hearts."

—John J. Pershing

Los Angeles National Cemetery,
Los Angeles, California

162

San Francisco National Cemetery, San Francisco, California

Mike Mullen
Excerpt from Remarks
at the 64th Annual
Pearl Harbor Day Commemoration

December 7, 2005
Pearl Harbor

I T IS A DISTINCT HONOR, AND A HUMBLING PRIVILEGE TO BE HERE. I SAY humbling because I know we stand in the company of men and women who remember this place not only as the beautiful paradise it is, but also as the bloody, unforgiving scene it once was. Men and women who remember all too well a fractured peace and a savage war.

... We must honor those who live with the reminders of what happened here, those who fought and survived the attack on Pearl Harbor. Those who recall the last moments of peace, and the first horrors of war, and the faces of fallen friends. That courageous few who can say, "I was at Pearl Harbor." To all the survivors here, thank you for being here....

Know that by your presence, you honor all who served here, those who can't be here, those who have passed on, and especially those who did not live to remember December 7 at all.

Sacramento Valley VA National
Cemetery, Sacramento, California

Your presence honors every act of bravery. The sailors who raced to their battle stations and opened fire on Japanese planes even as their ships were ablaze and sinking; men plunging into murky water to pull a shipmate to safety; rescuers racing their boats into the patches of

165

burning oil to snatch a sailor from a watery grave; a crew making a desperate dash down the channel. Pilots, who while vastly outnumbered took to the air to resist the enemy onslaught. After the order to abandon his capsizing ship, a young petty officer perishes holding a flashlight so others could see their way clear.

We also recognize the thousands of stories that will never be told; the letters home never finished; the deck watches never turned over; the homecomings never enjoyed.

In the Reserve, the National Guard, those citizen soldiers and sailors who stood ready when called, and in millions who immediately lined up and volunteered to join the fight, and fight they did.

GOLDEN GATE NATIONAL CEMETERY,
SAN BRUNO, CALIFORNIA

To all of those here from that Pearl Harbor generation, we are in your debt for the freedoms we enjoy today. And that legacy grows stronger with each passing year.

. . . Joshua Chamberlain, hero of the 20th Maine in the Battle of Gettysburg, was invited to return there some years later to dedicate a monument to the fallen men from his home state. Though he spoke about another fight in another time, of battlefields instead of battleships, Chamberlain captured in just a few words the sheer power of simply standing where something momentous had once occurred. He said, "In great deeds something abides. On great fields something stays. Forms change and pass, bodies disappear, but spirits linger to consecrate ground for the vision place of the soul. And reverent men and women from afar and generations that know us not, heart-drawn to see where and by whom great things were suffered and done for them, shall come here to ponder and to dream. And the power of the vision shall pass into their souls."

. . . God bless all of you who survived, those who did not, the families of all. God bless our navy and God bless our country. Thank you.

Los Angeles National Cemetery, Los Angeles, California

★ ★ ★

"Some people wonder all their lives if they've made a difference.

The marines don't have that problem."

—RONALD REAGAN

RIVERSIDE NATIONAL CEMETERY, RIVERSIDE, CALIFORNIA
(OPPOSITE): NATIONAL MEMORIAL CEMETERY OF ARIZONA, PHOENIX, ARIZONA

＊ ＊ ＊

*"They are surely to be esteemed the bravest spirits who, having the clearest sense
of both the pains and pleasures of life, do not on that account shrink from danger."*

—THUCYDIDES

169

Fort Logan National Cemetery, Denver, Colorado

SEAN HANNITY
EXCERPT FROM *LET FREEDOM RING*

WHAT IS AMAZING TO ME IS THE INCREDIBLE BRAVERY AND SACRIFICE of young people…who eagerly go to war against…murderous lunatics, joining our armed forces and the CIA and taking up arms in the defense of liberty and their fellow countrymen. Even though it may cost them everything they have to give.

Such commitment, in the face of such grave danger, requires a measure of love and devotion to country that only the finest among us can truly muster. And when we see people make these kinds of commitments—and pay the ultimate price, with the currency of their own blood—it is our duty to them, their families, those who have gone before them, and those who will follow, to honor them. Thank them. And lift them up as models for us and our children to follow. For such men and women represent the best America has to offer. And we dare not forget them.

EAGLE POINT NATIONAL CEMETERY,
EAGLE POINT, OREGON

…I want to conclude…by simply thanking God that our military remains the best in the world and by thanking the brave men and women who serve in our armed forces and put their lives on the line each and every day. To all who wear the uniform of our country—in the army, air force, marines, and coast guard—let me just say:

Thank you for all that you do, for putting yourself in harm's way so that your fellow countrymen can remain free and safe.

Fort Rosecrans National Cemetery, San Diego, California

National Memorial Cemetery of the Pacific, Honolulu, Hawaii

ETERNAL FATHER,
STRONG TO SAVE

✳ ✳ ✳

Eternal Father, Lord of hosts,

Watch o'er the men who guard our coasts.

Protect them from the raging seas

And give them light and life and peace.

Grant them from thy great throne above

The shield and shelter of thy love.

—*George H. Jenks, Jr., USCG (1955)*

FREEDOM ALLIANCE SCHOLARSHIP FUND

Supporting the Children
of America's Military Heroes

THE FREEDOM ALLIANCE SCHOLARSHIP FUND HONORS THE BRAVERY AND dedication of Americans in our armed forces who have sacrificed life or limb by providing college scholarships to their children. Through the generosity of the American public, the Scholarship Fund has awarded more than $1 million to the sons and daughters of American heroes.

Many of freedom's brave defenders have lost their lives fighting terrorism and defending our nation. These were good men and women who loved their country, and no doubt their dying thoughts were for their beloved families back home. There are few things in life more difficult than having to tell a grieving wife about the loss of her husband and then watch as she tells her kids that their daddy will never again come home.

At Freedom Alliance, we know that the good people of this country won't let our military families grieve alone. Through the Freedom Alliance Scholarship Fund, we show our support for our fallen heroes by helping their children meet the rising cost of a college education, and in so doing, we remind them that their parents' sacrifice will never be forgotten by a grateful nation.

The Origins of the National Cemetery Administration

"To care for him who shall have borne the battle and for his widow, and for his orphan."

—Abraham Lincoln

T HE DEPARTMENT OF VETERANS AFFAIRS NATIONAL CEMETERY ADMINIS-tration honors veterans with final resting places in national shrines and provides lasting tributes that commemorate their military service to our nation; a mission of privilege and honor.

On July 17, 1862, Congress enacted legislation that authorized President Lincoln "to purchase cemetery grounds, and cause them to be securely enclosed, to be used as a national cemetery for soldiers who shall die in the service of the country." Fourteen cemeteries were established that first year.

By 1870, the remains of nearly 300,000 Union dead had been buried in seventy-three national cemeteries. Most of the cemeteries were located in the Southeast, near the battlefields and campgrounds of the Civil War.

The National Cemetery Administration has evolved since the initial period related to the Civil War. In 1873, all honorably discharged veterans became eligible for burial. In the 1930s, new national cemeteries were established to serve veterans living in major metropolitan areas such as New York, Baltimore, Minneapolis, San Diego, San Francisco, and San Antonio.

In 1973, Congress transferred eighty-two national cemeteries from the Department of the Army to the Veterans Administration, now the Department of Veterans Affairs (VA). These were added to the twenty-one VA cemeteries at hospitals and nursing homes to comprise 103 cemeteries in what was then the VA's National Cemetery System.

On November 11, 1998, the Veterans Programs Enhancement Act was signed, changing the name of the National Cemetery System to the National Cemetery Administration.

Today, there are a total of 141 national cemeteries. The VA's National Cemetery Administration is responsible for 125 of them, while the National Park Service maintains fourteen and the Department of the Army maintains two cemeteries, including Arlington National Cemetery.

VA is experiencing the largest cemetery expansion since the Civil War, and currently operates 125 national cemeteries in thirty-nine states and Puerto Rico. Their newest national cemeteries, Georgia National Cemetery and Sacramento Valley VA National Cemetery, opened in 2006, and South Florida VA National Cemetery opened in 2007. VA is keeping its commitment to America's veterans by opening additional cemeteries in Sarasota and Jacksonville, FL; Bakersfield, CA; Birmingham, AL; Philadelphia, PA; and Columbia, SC. More than three million Americans, including veterans of every war and conflict—from the Revolutionary War to the global War on Terror—are buried in the VA's national cemeteries.

These oaths and promises of caring for our nation's veterans are kept every day by the men and women of VA's National Cemetery Administration, most of whom are themselves veterans.

LIST OF PHOTOGRAPHERS

This book would not have been possible without the generous
donations of the following photographers:

Dave Au

Brendan Bailey

Frank Bailey

Lt. David and Addison Barker

Christine Buie

Sinde Butler

Jim Cecil

Walter Chilenski

Lauren Cromwell

Daniel Dyer

Eris Filoberto

Lisa Fry

Nanette Furio

Jeannine Happ

Sandy and Clint Hedgepeth

Phil and Margaret Hitchcock

Meriel Jones

Rochelle Kasseus

Patrick McElhenney

Shaun McGrath

John Miller

National Cemetery Administration

Gary Nichols

Ted Richardson

Michelle Schmitt

Don Seto

Teri Stanley

D.J. Stewart

Ryan Terpay

B.B. Yarborough

Dirk Yarborough

PHOTOGRAPHY CREDITS

Dave Au
141 (top), 156

Brendan Bailey
66

Frank Bailey
79, 84

Lt. David and Addison Barker
22, 25, 40

Christine Buie
vi, 9, 13, 19, 28 (bottom), 32, 36, 39

Sinde Butler
139, 142-143, 146, 150-151, 162-163,
167, 168

Jim Cecil
126, 141 (bottom), 144, 148, 171

Walter Chilenski
86, 92, 101, 108, 109, 112 (top), 119

Lauren Cromwell
90, 97, 100, 112 (bottom), 123 (top), 124

Daniel Dyer
133, 152, 157, 161

Eris Filoberto
46, 51, 54, 55, 61, 63, 80

Lisa Fry
136, 138, 145, 149, 153, 155, 170

Nanette Furio
57, 73 (bottom)

Jeannine Happ
134-135, 140, 147, 164, 166

Sandy Hedgepeth
2, 18, 33, 37 (top)

Clint Hedgepeth
43

Phil and Margaret Hitchcock
88-89, 94, 98-99, 106-107, 110, 113,
114-115, 120, 122

Meriel Jones
17, 29, 37 (bottom)

Rochelle Kasseus
60, 78 (bottom)

Patrick McElhenney
48, 56, 62, 70, 78 (top), 83

Shaun McGrath
158-159

John Miller
38

National Cemetery Administration
6, 21, 31, 35, 50, 67, 71, 72, 73 (top),
81, 82, 93 (top), 95, 103, 121,
123 (bottom), 165

Gary Nichols
4-5, 8, 12, 20, 28 (top), 34

Ted Richardson
10-11, 16, 24, 42

Michelle Schmitt
93 (bottom), 102, 104, 118

Don Seto
132, 137, 154, 160, 174

Teri Stanley
49, 52-53, 58-59, 64, 68-69, 75

D.J. Stewart
116

Ryan Terpay
14-15, 23, 26-27, 44

B.B. Yarborough
128-129, 169, 172-173

Dirk Yarborough
x, 130

Acknowledgments

I WANT TO EXPRESS MY APPRECIATION AND GRATITUDE TO ALL THOSE WHO, without their help and guidance, this book would not have become all that it is.

To each and every photographer who battled the elements, adjusting work schedules and driving great distances to capture the beauty and dignity of our national cemeteries. Without your efforts, this book would not be here today.

To Jim Riordan of Seven Locks Press who was the first in the industry to embrace the value and importance of this book and who never faltered in his commitment that made this dream come true.

Thank you to each and every person at Regnery Publishing for your contribution in making this project a reality. You demonstrated professionalism, commitment, and belief in the American dream. The American way of life is alive and well and will continue to thrive as long as there are corporations like Regnery Publishing. My personal thanks to: Marji Ross, president and publisher; John Lalor, director of sales and custom publishing; Alex Novak, director of marketing; Amanda Larsen, art director; and a special thank you to my editor, Kate Frantz.

To the National Cemetery Administration who granted permission for this project and without whose approval, this book would not exist today. A very special thanks to Under Secretary for Memorial Affairs William Tuerk, Director of Communication Management David Schettler, Chief of Communications and Outreach Support Mike Nacincik, and Jurita Barber, public affairs officer, for taking on this project.

And special thanks to Senator Dole and Miriam Brioso.

Dee Wilgenbusch and Tom Kilgannon at the Freedom Alliance Foundation for understanding what the loss of a parent means to a child and working hard to make sure these children will know that America will never forget the sacrifice of their parent.

Without the guidance and direction from Johnny Grant, Margaret Burk, and the late Ward Grant, the success of this project would not have reached the level of achievement it has. Thank you!

Thank you to each and every celebrity and their management team for understanding the essence of this project: Linda Hope, Donna Ellis, and Annette Siegel at the Bob Hope offices; Kathryn Sermak and Buzz Aldrin; Sean Hannity; Laura Ingraham; Alan Margulies and Ann-Margret; Paul Shef and Dennis Miller; Marsha Fishbaugh and Lt. Col. Oliver North; Kevin Pawley and Mickey and Jan Rooney; Jennifer Weyent and Paul Teutul, Sr.; Lois and Fred Travalena.

To Mr. Carlos Lopes, general manager for the Hotel Bel Air and to his remarkable staff in their lounge where this book was created. To Antonio Castillo, who works his magic on the piano, Steve Conlin, master of mixology, Bruno Lopez, whose food creations are beyond belief, especially Erik Orozco, Krystina Benck, and Britt Morrow, who greet everyone so warmly and make you feel like you are family on every visit, thank you!

My entire family who, each in their own way, has helped and encouraged me especially at the beginning when there were nothing but closed doors and unreturned phone calls. To two fine gentlement who supported this project from the start, Denver "DJ," who actually shot photos for this book, and Travis whom I am so proud to say is a member of the U.S. Army Reserve. To my sister, Sandy, and her husband, Col. Jack Bauman, (USAF, Ret), who listened to this concept and told me to "go for it, we support you all the way," and they so lovingly did.

To my niece, Anne, and her husband, Keith, who were so supportive during the whole process. Anne was my number one fan for this book. She believed in this book honoring our soldiers and their families from the start and was determined that I would succeed. Thank you.

And to each person listed below, I thank you for your help and support. You will never know how much everything you have done means to our troops and their families.

Col. Jeffrey Buczkowski,
U.S. Army Master Sergeant

Karl Angelo

Karen Brown

David Burke

Brad "Martini" Chambers

Tom Fuentes

Stephanie Davidson

Steve Skaggs

Bob Williams

Ryan Yantis

Robyn Killian

Sonya Mirande

Lisa Beth Snyder,
U.S. Army

Jerry Jacobson

Paul Mast

Dr. Terry McGee

Don Morrison

Jean & Ed Poole

Dan Rodgers

Ed Grady

Dean Judkins

Debra Lowther

Bruce Zielsdorf

Dr. Murray Lappe

To every American, thank you for your support of our veterans, and because of all of you, their sacred ground will never be forgotten. God bless you!

INDEX